1001
Animals to Spot

Ruth Brocklehurst
Illustrated by Teri Gower

Designed by Susannah Owen

Edited by Anna Milbourne

Natural history consultant: Dr. Margaret Rostron

For every book sold, the illustrator will make a donation to
Care for the Wild International.

Contents

Animals to spot

The pictures in this book show animals living all around the world. In each picture there are animals for you to find and count.

There are 1001 animals to spot altogether. The example pages below show what you need to do to find them.

Each little picture shows you what to look for in the big picture.

The blue number tells you how many of that animal you need to spot.

This is Leo the artist. He draws animals everywhere he goes. See if you can spot his drawing pad and pencil in each scene.

On pages 30 and 31 there are two more puzzles for you to do.

On the farm

3 puppies 5 ducks 9 ducklings 8 black lambs 10 black and white lambs

4

6 hens

4 brown foals

10 chicks

6 cows

10 calves

On safari

10 ostriches　　4 hippos　　5 lion cubs　　4 elephants　　6 giraffes

6 rhinos   10 zebras   8 vultures   9 warthogs   10 gazelles

In the desert

10 black ants

4 rattlesnakes

8 scorpions

10 tarantulas

9 painted grasshoppers

6 woodpeckers

4 jack rabbits

5 tortoises

7 gila monsters

3 coyotes

In the Arctic

10 caribou

4 polar bears

10 seals

6 snowy owls

9 lemmings

1 humpback whale

6 Arctic foxes

4 killer whales

8 baby seals

5 narwhals

In the woods

10 blue butterflies

7 rabbits

9 blackbirds

2 badgers

10 squirrels

12

8 wood pigeons   7 deer   10 hedgehogs   5 foxes   10 shrews

In the ocean

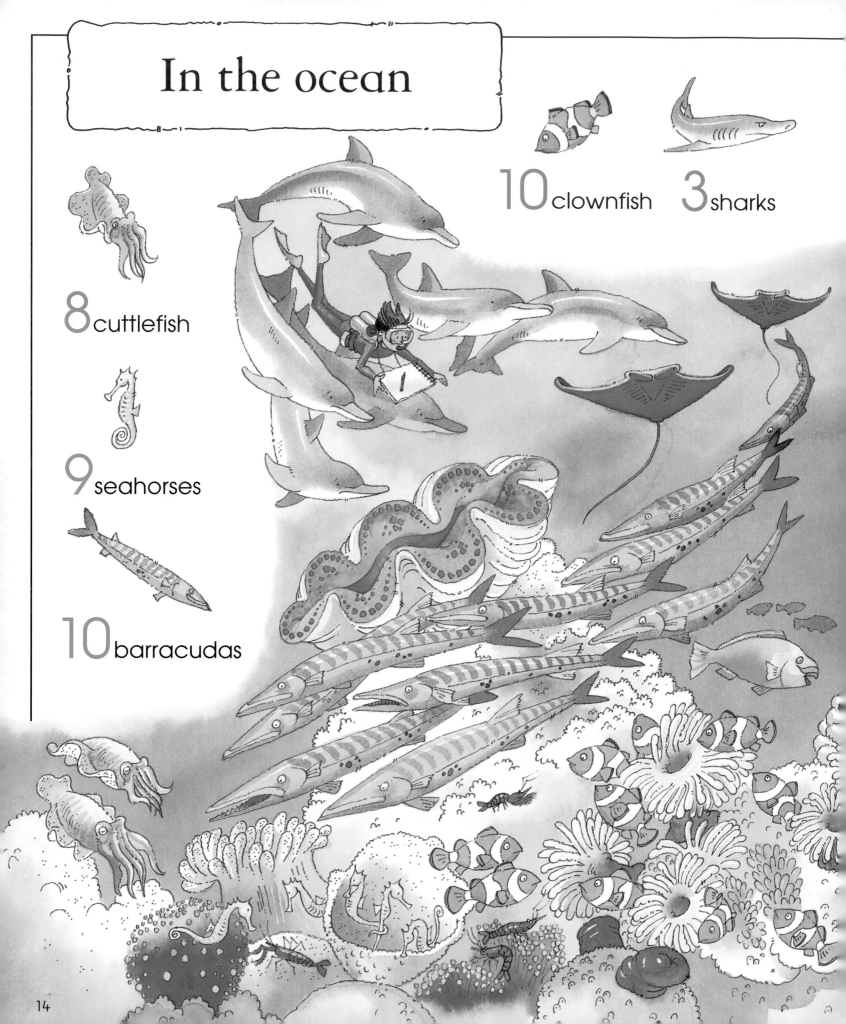

10 clownfish   3 sharks

8 cuttlefish

9 seahorses

10 barracudas

8 shrimps   3 manta rays   10 snappers   6 dolphins   7 parrotfish

In the rainforest

5 sloths

7 arrow-poison frogs

8 toucans

3 coral snakes

1 jaguar

9 parrots

7 spider monkeys

10 egrets

5 armadillos

8 boas

In the garden

7 moths   10 mice   6 green caterpillars   8 spiders   8 sparrows

10 bees   9 snails   2 kittens   8 starlings   6 worms

In the outback

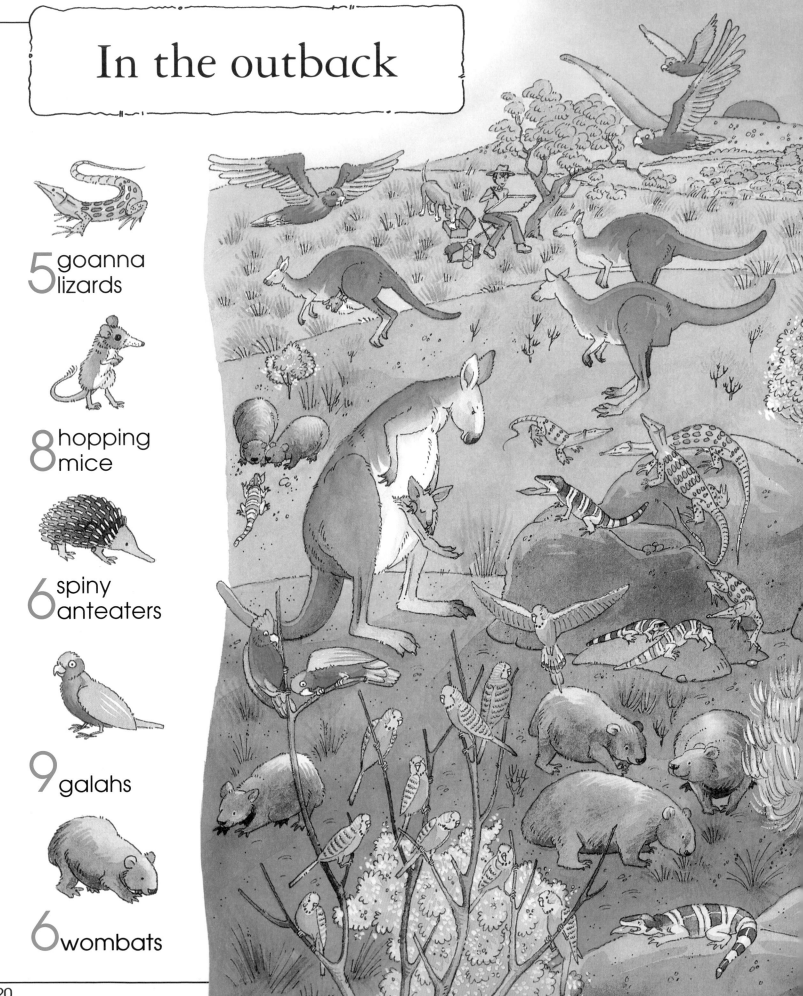

5 goanna lizards

8 hopping mice

6 spiny anteaters

9 galahs

6 wombats

8 kangaroos

5 joeys

4 dingoes

10 emus

10 parakeets

In the swamp

1 alligator 7 herons 10 bullfrogs 1 manatee 5 woodpeckers

8 newts   10 apple snails   10 dragonflies   9 turtles   9 grasshoppers

In the mountains

10 butterflies 9 pikas

9 mountain goats

5 eagles

10 geese   7 marmots   3 vultures   1 snow leopard   3 black bears

5 yaks

By the sea

5 oystercatchers

10 mussels

6 crabs

8 seagulls

6 sea urchins

6 seals 5 squat lobsters 10 winkles 10 limpets 7 sea anemones

Children's farm

5 peacocks 9 doves 6 llamas 8 hens 7 goats

28

10 ducks

5 Shetland ponies

10 guinea pigs

3 camels

10 rabbits

Leo's pictures

Here are some pictures of animals that Leo drew on his travels. Look back through the book and see if you can find and count them all.

6 otters

9 scarlet ibises

5 magpies

10 wildebeests

7 blue-tongued skinks

9 puffins

10 hairy caterpillars

3 giant clams

9 red ants

10 wallcreepers

4 turkeys

10 walruses